A Day with Police Officers

by Jodie Shepherd

Content Consultant
Chief Douglas Fuchs, Redding, Connecticut Police Department

Reading Consultant
Jeanne Clidas, Ph.D.
Reading Specialist

Children's Press®
An Imprint of Scholastic Inc.
New York Toronto London Auckland Sydney
Mexico City New Delhi Hong Kong
Danbury, Connecticut

Library of Congress Cataloging-in-Publication Data
Shepherd, Jodie.
  A day with police officers / by Jodie Shepherd.
    p. cm. — (Rookie read-about community)
  Includes index.
  ISBN 978-0-531-28955-6 (library binding) — ISBN 978-0-531-29255-6 (pbk.)
1. Police—Juvenile literature. I. Title.
HV7922.S49 2013
363.2—dc23   2012013352

Produced by Spooky Cheetah Press

4 5 6 7 8 9 10 R 22 21 20 19 18 17 16 15 14

Photographs © 2013: Alamy Images/Pat Canova: 27; Corbis Images/Mark
Peterson: 11; Getty Images/Theo Wargo: 7; Media Bakery/Charlie Schuck: 28;
Shutterstock, Inc.: 15 (Anne Kitzman), 12 (Barry Blackburn), 3 bottom (Eric Isselée),
23 (Jose Gil), 19 (Michael Rubin), 3 top left (Stephen Mulcahey), 3 top right
(Volodymyr Krasyuk); Thaddeus Harden: 8, 24; Thinkstock: 20, 31 bottom left, 31 top
right (Hemera), 31 top left (iStockphoto), 16 (Jupiterimages/Getty Images), cover,
4, 31 bottom right (Siri Stafford).

Table of Contents

hat

radio

badge

patch

shoes

4

Meet a Police Officer

When you see police officers, they are hard at work. What do they do?

Here to Help!

Police officers help people who are in **trouble**. If you are lost, a police officer will help you.

Police officers make sure
people follow the rules, or laws.
They help to keep grown-ups and
children safe.

Police officers keep **neighborhoods** safe, too.

11

Stop and Go

Some police officers help with traffic. They direct cars, trucks, and buses on busy streets.

A red light means stop! Police officers make sure drivers follow the rules of the road. This is a way to keep people safe.

15

Watch out! A person who does not follow the rules may get a ticket.

On the Move

Police officers move from place to place when they work. Sometimes they walk. Sometimes they ride bicycles.

Sometimes they drive police cars. If you hear a police **siren**, get out of the way. A police officer is rushing to help someone.

Police officers can even travel by scooter or motorcycle.

Animal Partners

Some police officers have an animal **partner**, such as a horse. Up on a horse, it is easy to see all around.

Dogs make great partners, too. Police dogs are good at sniffing out trouble. They are also good at finding people who are lost.

Just Ask!

If you need help, just ask a police officer!

Try It! Look at the picture of the police officer on page 4. Point to the parts of his uniform—his badge and the patch on his sleeve—that let you know he is someone you can go to for help.

Be a Community Helper!

- Follow the rules. That makes a police officer's job easier!

- If you see something that does not look right, tell a police officer.

- Let police officers do their jobs. If they are busy, get out of their way. Do not pet police dogs unless a police officer says it is okay.

- Thank your neighborhood police officers for the work they do.

Words You Know

dog

horse

police car

police officer

31

Index

Facts for Now

Visit this Scholastic Web site for more information on police officers:
www.factsfornow.scholastic.com
Enter the keywords **Police Officers**

About the Author

Jodie Shepherd, who also writes under the name Leslie Kimmelman, is an award-winning author of dozens of books for children, both fiction and nonfiction. She is also a children's book editor.